Spotter's Guide to
DINOSAURS
& other prehistoric animals

David Norman
Lecturer in Zoology, London University

Illustrated by Bob Hersey

HAMILTON
COLLEGE

Contents

Designed and edited by
Ruth Thomson

Series editor
Bridget Gibbs

Additional artwork by
Cloud Nine Design
and Andy Martin

First published in 1980 by
Usborne Publishing Limited,
20 Garrick Street, London WC2

© 1980 by Usborne Publishing Limited

Published in Australia by Rigby
Publishing Ltd, Adelaide, Sydney,
Melbourne, Brisbane.
Printed and bound in Great Britain by
Morrison & Gibb Ltd, London and Edinburgh

How to use this book

This book is an illustrated guide to dinosaurs and other animals to which they are related. Take it with you when you go to a Natural History Museum. Many museums have fossil skeletons of dinosaurs or examples of their skulls, teeth or bones. The pictures in this book will help you realize what the living animals probably looked like.

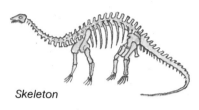

Skeleton

The main section of the book deals with dinosaurs. These are a special group of reptiles, all of which are now extinct. There are also sections on other animals which lived before, during or after the time of the dinosaurs. There are tips on fossil collecting and examples of common fossils.

Reconstructed model

What the illustrations show

People who study dinosaurs and other fossils try to put together fossil bones, for example those of a dinosaur, to make a complete skeleton. The shape and arrangement of bones makes it possible to discover the shape of its body, how it moved (quickly or slowly) and whether it walked on two legs or four. They can tell from its teeth whether it was a meat- or a plant-eater. The only thing they cannot tell at all is the colour of its skin. All the animals in this book are shown as they might have looked, based on the evidence people have found; the colours, however, are imaginary.

Time scale

At the end of each caption in the sections on dinosaurs and their relatives, you will see a time scale like the one below. The blue shaded area shows when that particular animal lived. Geologists have divided the millions of years since life began into four Eras. Each Era is divided into Periods. Dinosaurs and their relatives lived between 225 and 64 million years ago in the Mesozoic Era. This is divided into three Periods – Triassic, Jurassic and Cretaceous.

Triassic	Jurassic		Cretaceous
225	195	135	*Millions of years ago* 64

How to use this book

Measurements

All the dinosaurs and their relatives are measured from head to tail. This measurement is known as their body length (BL).

Body length (BL)

None of the dinosaurs is drawn to scale. To help give you some idea of their sizes there is a scale box beside each illustration. These show how the size of a particular dinosaur compares with a familiar animal or, for the really large dinosaurs, with a container lorry.

Some are compared with a mallard duck (body length 60cm).

Some are compared with a giraffe (body length 4-5 m).

Some are compared with a zebra (body length 2-2.5 m).

Some are compared with an elephant (body length 6-7.5 m).

Some are compared with a crocodile (body length 4 m).

The biggest dinosaurs are compared with a container lorry (15 m).

Names and places

Many of the dinosaurs and their relatives have names which end with *–saurus*. This word comes from the Greek and literally means "lizard". It is, however, more meaningfully translated as "reptile". Most names describe a particular characteristic of the animal concerned; dinosaur, for example, means "terrible reptile". In this book, the translated name is given in italics under the scientific name.

There is also a pronunciation guide under the name of each animal to help you say the word. It is written like this:
(Tee-lee-oh-saw-rus)
The part of the word that is underlined is the one to emphasize.

At the end of each animal description is the name of one or more countries or continents. This tells you where the fossils of each one were found.

Continental Drift

The continents of the earth may seem firm and solid but, in fact, they are moving all the time (although very slowly – perhaps a few centimetres a year). Over millions of years the continents have moved quite considerably. This movement is called Continental Drift.

If you look, for example, at the coastlines of North and South America and of Africa and Europe, it is clear that these great land masses could fit together like jigsaw pieces. 200 million years ago they did, in fact, fit together neatly. Since then, they have been pushed apart gradually and today they are separated by the Atlantic Ocean.

Recent studies of the ocean floors have shown that there are a series of deep cracks (known as trenches) and mountain chains (known as ridges) which divide the surface of the earth into enormous plates (called tectonic plates). The land masses float on these great plates and are moved by them. The plates are moving continually. At the ridges, molten rock rises up from the hot centre of the earth to the surface; as it does so, it cools.

Position of mid-oceanic ridge

Some of this rock spreads out sideways forming new ocean floor, so the plates are pushed outwards from these ridges.

Since the earth is not growing larger, there must also be areas where sea floor is disappearing. This happens at the oceanic trenches. At these places, two tectonic plates are pushing against each other and one plate slips beneath the other and re-enters the hot mantle. At present, most of the trenches are found around the edges of the Pacific Ocean.

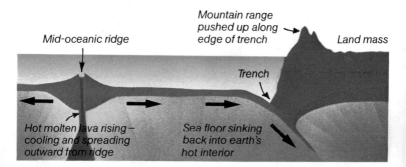

Mid-oceanic ridge

Mountain range pushed up along edge of trench

Land mass

Trench

Hot molten lava rising – cooling and spreading outward from ridge

Sea floor sinking back into earth's hot interior

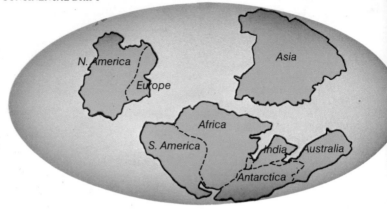

1. Palaeozoic Era (between 600 and 225 million years ago)

The movements of the continents during this time are not very well known. There appear to have been at least three large continental blocks: Europe and North America, Asia, and a third comprising all the remaining continents (South America, Africa, Antarctica, Australia and India).

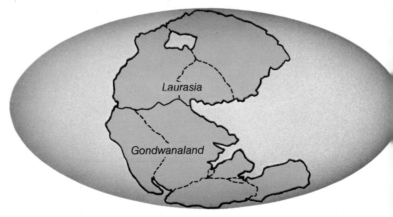

2. Triassic Period (between 225 and 195 million years ago)

By this time, the three original continental blocks were joined together in a single, huge supercontinent called Pangaea. This consisted of two major land masses – a northern one, called Laurasia, and a southern one, called Gondwanaland. Reptiles spread throughout this uninterrupted supercontinent.

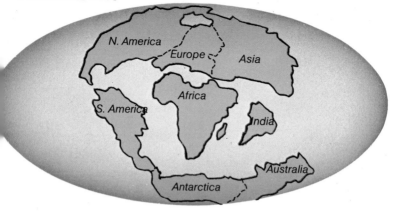

3. Cretaceous Period (between 135 and 64 million years ago)

In the Jurassic Period, Pangaea started to split up. Gondwanaland began to separate from Laurasia. They were completely separate in Early Cretaceous times.

By the end of the Cretaceous Period, Gondwanaland was breaking up into recognizable continents – South America, Africa, India, Antarctica and Australia.

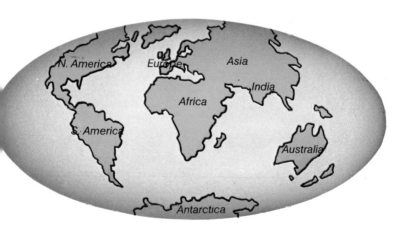

4. Recent (from 64 million years ago to the present time)

The continental blocks continued to divide and separate from one another. Eventually they settled into their present-day positions.

One of the last separations that took place was that between North America and Europe.

Time chart

Era	Period		Climate			

Era	Period	Climate		
Mesozoic	Cretaceous	64	Cool	Age of Reptiles
		135	Warm/Wet	
	Jurassic		Warm	
		195		
	Triassic	225	Warm/Dry	
Palaeozoic	Permian	280	Warm/Dry	
	Carboniferous		Tropical	
		345	Glacial at South Pole	
	Devonian	395	Warm/Dry	Age of Fish
	Silurian	440	Warm	
	Ordovician	500	Cool/Warm	
	Cambrian	600	Cold	

Time millions of years ago

Birds
Ornithomimus
Tyrannosaurus
Deinonychus
Archaeopteryx
Compsognathus
Ceratosa
Mammals
?
Megazostrodon
Coelop
Amphibians
Diplocaulus
Seymouria
Eusthenop
Cephalaspis
Cup Coral
Hallucigenia

8

This time chart shows how dinosaurs are related to one another and to some other prehistoric animals. All dinosaurs are descendants of a group of primitive archosaur reptiles (see page 18), which are represented in this chart by Euparkeria and Chasmatosaurus.

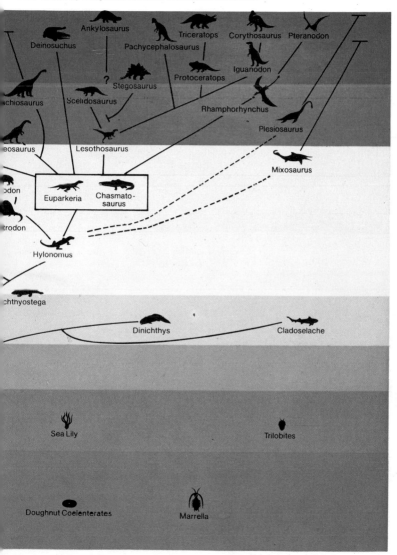

Deinosuchus
Ankylosaurus
Pachycephalosaurus
Triceratops
Corythosaurus
Pteranodon
chiosaurus
Scelidosaurus
?
Stegosaurus
Protoceratops
Iguanodon
Rhamphorhynchus
eosaurus
Lesothosaurus
Plesiosaurus
Mixosaurus
odon
Euparkeria
Chasmato-
saurus
trodon
Hylonomus
chthyostega
Dinichthys
Cladoselache
Sea Lily
Trilobites
Doughnut Coelenterates
Marrella

Dinosaur family tree

Dinosaurs are divided into two quite distinct groups (or Orders) – the "lizard-hipped" (known as the Saurischia) and the "bird-hipped" (known as the Ornithischia).

Lizard-hipped (Saurischia)

These dinosaurs have hip bones arranged much like other reptiles. There are three bones in the hip. The one above the hip socket is called the ilium. The one below it, which points forwards and downwards, is called the pubis. The other, which points backwards and downwards, is called the ischium.

Bird-hipped (Ornithischia)

The arrangement of these dinosaurs' hip bones resembles that of birds. The ilium and ischium are in the same position. The pubis points backwards and downwards and lies beneath the ischium. Later types of "bird-hipped" dinosaurs developed an extra piece of bone on the pubis, which pointed forwards.

All "bird-hipped" dinosaurs had a bone, called the predentary, at the tip of their bottom jaw and thin bony rods supporting their backbone. "Lizard-hipped" dinosaurs had neither.

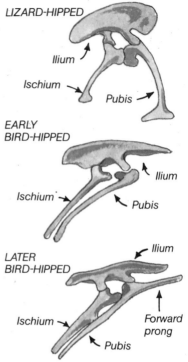

LIZARD-HIPPED

Ilium
Ischium
Pubis

EARLY BIRD-HIPPED

Ischium
Ilium
Pubis

LATER BIRD-HIPPED

Ilium
Ischium
Forward prong
Pubis

Skull of Heterodontosaurus

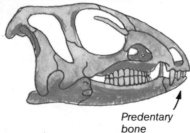

Predentary bone

You can see on this chart which kinds of dinosaur belong to each group. There were two main types of "lizard-hipped" ones: enormous plant-eaters that walked on all fours (called sauropods and prosauropods), and meat-eaters that walked on two legs (called theropods).

Two-legged ornithopods were the first "bird-hipped" dinosaurs. Others were the horned dinosaurs (ceratopians), plated dinosaurs (stegosaurs) and armoured dinosaurs (ankylosaurs). All "bird-hipped" dinosaurs were plant-eaters.

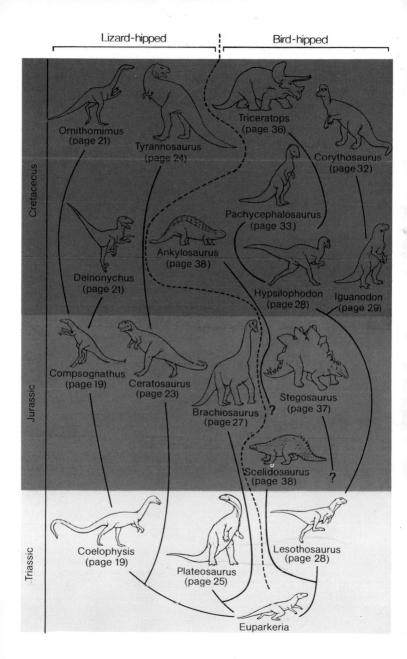

Lizard-hipped | Bird-hipped

Cretaceous

Ornithomimus (page 21)

Tyrannosaurus (page 24)

Triceratops (page 36)

Corythosaurus (page 32)

Pachycephalosaurus (page 33)

Deinonychus (page 21)

Ankylosaurus (page 38)

Hypsilophodon (page 28)

Iguanodon (page 29)

Jurassic

Compsognathus (page 19)

Ceratosaurus (page 23)

Brachiosaurus (page 27)

Stegosaurus (page 37)

?

Scelidosaurus (page 38)

?

Triassic

Coelophysis (page 19)

Plateosaurus (page 25)

Lesothosaurus (page 28)

Euparkeria

How fossils are formed

A dinosaur dies and its body sinks into a lake.

Its flesh gradually rots away, leaving only its skeleton.

Slowly, over thousands of years, the skeleton petrifies.

A fossil is the remains of an animal or plant preserved in rocks. Dinosaurs are one of the many groups of extinct animals known about only from their fossils.

Dinosaurs lived on land, although a few may have lived in swamps or around lakes and rivers. When a dinosaur died, whether killed by another dinosaur or through illness or old age, its body lay on the ground. There, it was either eaten by a flesh-eating animal, which crushed and scattered its bones, or it merely rotted away. In either case, all remains of the dinosaur vanished without trace.

If, however, a dinosaur died near a river or swamp it was quite likely to be preserved. Its body sank into the muddy waters of the swamp or was washed down river and buried in the silt at the bottom of the lake. Its soft flesh gradually rotted away, leaving the hard, bony skeleton covered in mud.

Over thousands more years, more and more layers of mud built up on top of the skeleton. Eventually, the enormous weight of these layers compressed the mud into rock.

Throughout this time, water seeped through the rocks. It contained small amounts of chemicals and minerals. These filled all the minute holes in the bones of the skeleton. This made them extremely heavy.

Eventually, the whole bone was replaced by the minerals, which slowly solidified into stone. The solidified minerals stay in the same shape as the original bone. This process is called petrification.

The rock containing the fossil weathers and the fossil is found.

The rock is cut away so that the fossil can be removed for study.

Throughout the history of the earth, its surface (known as the crust) has been slowly moving – lifting, sinking, bending, folding and buckling. As it has moved, so the layers of rock containing fossils have also moved. After thousands, or even millions, of years some of these layers of rock containing dinosaur skeletons have been heaved up into the air to form dry land.

Weathering by wind, rain or the sea gradually wears away the rocks to uncover fossilized skeletons. Sometimes people uncover fossils when digging in mines or quarries or preparing foundations for new buildings. If a fossil is not discovered soon after being exposed then it, too, gradually weathers away to dust and is lost forever.

On very rare occasions, other sorts of dinosaur fossils are found. These may be teeth, eggs, footprint tracks, impressions of skin or even droppings.

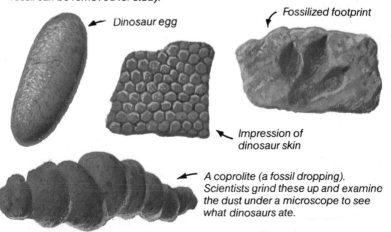

Dinosaur egg

Fossilized footprint

Impression of dinosaur skin

A coprolite (a fossil dropping). Scientists grind these up and examine the dust under a microscope to see what dinosaurs ate.

Early fossils

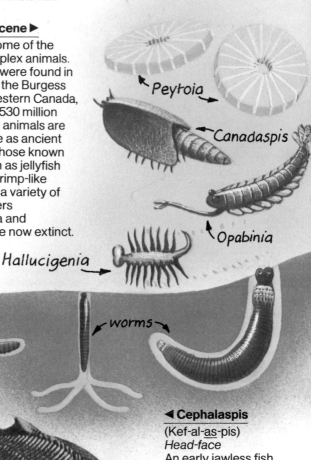

Cambrian scene ▶

These are some of the earliest complex animals. Their fossils were found in rocks called the Burgess Shales in Western Canada, dating back 530 million years. Some animals are recognizable as ancient relatives of those known today – such as jellyfish (Peytoia), shrimp-like animals and a variety of worms. Others (Hallucigenia and Opabinia) are now extinct.

Peytoia

Canadaspis

Opabinia

Hallucigenia

worms

worm

◀ Cephalaspis

(Kef-al-<u>as</u>-pis)
Head-face
An early jawless fish. Heavily armoured against attack by giant sea "scorpions" which were common at this time. Sucked food particles, in mud on sea floor, through slit on underside of head. Europe. N. America. BL 30 cm.

eyes on top of head

Jawed fish

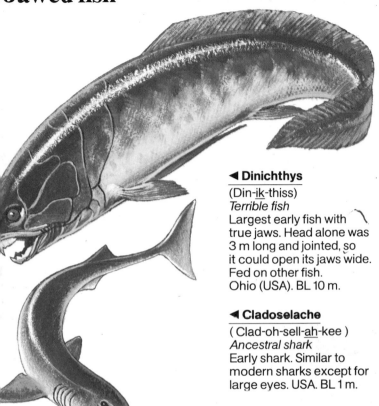

◀ Dinichthys

(Din-ik-thiss)
Terrible fish
Largest early fish with
true jaws. Head alone was
3 m long and jointed, so
it could open its jaws wide.
Fed on other fish.
Ohio (USA). BL 10 m.

◀ Cladoselache

(Clad-oh-sell-ah-kee)
Ancestral shark
Early shark. Similar to
modern sharks except for
large eyes. USA. BL 1 m.

Eusthenopteron ▶

(Yews-then-op-tur-on)
True narrow fin
Fierce, bony freshwater
fish. Had lungs to breathe
air as well as gills. Its
muscular fins could be
used like legs on land.
Greenland. BL 1 m.

thick
muscular
base to fins

Amphibians

Amphibians can walk on land and breathe air, but they cannot live on dry land all the time. They need to return to water to lay their soft, jelly-covered eggs.

Ichthyostega ▶
(Ik-thee-oh-<u>stee</u>-ga)
Fish roof
First land vertebrate. Had fish-like body, scales on belly, fin on tail and sharp, pointed teeth. Could walk on land with its strong legs, but lived mainly in water and ate fish. Greenland. BL 1 m.

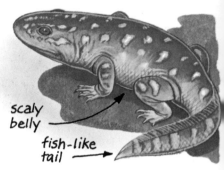

scaly belly

fish-like tail

horns

◀ Diplocaulus
(Dip-low-<u>cawl</u>-us)
Double stalk
Had a flattened body, small legs and a long tail for swimming. Its horns were probably used as stabilizers for swimming in fast-flowing streams. Texas. BL 80 cm.

Seymouria ▶
(See-<u>more</u>-ee-a)
From Seymour (Texas)
Long thought to be a reptile. Its relatives are now known to have laid eggs in water, which hatched as tadpoles. It lived mainly on land. USA. BL 80 cm.

powerful legs

Early reptiles

Reptiles evolved from amphibians. They were able to live on land permanently because they could lay eggs covered by a shell, which did not dry out.

Hylonomus ▶
(<u>Hy</u>-lon-<u>oh</u>-mus)
In-trcc mouse
One of the first reptiles.
Had lizard-like body with
scaly skin. Ate insects.
Nova Scotia. BL 10-20 cm.

Dimetrodon ▶
(Dee-<u>mee</u>-tro-don)
Two-sized tooth
Flesh-eater with sharp
teeth. "Sail" on back
helped control body
temperature. USA. BL 3 m.

large sail

two tusks

◀ Dicynodon
(Dy-<u>sin</u>-oh-don)
Two-dog tooth
Pig-shaped. Toothless
apart from two tusks in top
jaw. Nibbled plants with
beak. S. Africa. BL 1 m.

◀ Lycaenops
(<u>Ly</u>-sun-ops) *Wolf-face*
Fierce flesh eater. Slim,
scaly body. Long legs for
chasing prey, and sharp
teeth. S. Africa. BL 1.5 m.

Archosaurs

One particular group of reptiles, called archosaurs, appeared in late Permian times (230 million years ago). At first they were large, crocodile-like animals with bony armour and heavy tails. Later, they evolved into the dinosaurs.

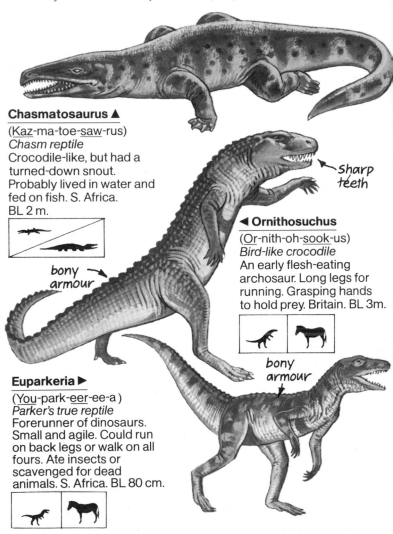

Chasmatosaurus ▲

(<u>Kaz</u>-ma-toe-<u>saw</u>-rus)
Chasm reptile
Crocodile-like, but had a
turned-down snout.
Probably lived in water and
fed on fish. S. Africa.
BL 2 m.

bony
armour

sharp
teeth

◀ Ornithosuchus

(<u>Or</u>-nith-oh-<u>sook</u>-us)
Bird-like crocodile
An early flesh-eating
archosaur. Long legs for
running. Grasping hands
to hold prey. Britain. BL 3m.

bony
armour

Euparkeria ▶

(<u>You</u>-park-<u>eer</u>-ee-a)
Parker's true reptile
Forerunner of dinosaurs.
Small and agile. Could run
on back legs or walk on all
fours. Ate insects or
scavenged for dead
animals. S. Africa. BL 80 cm.

Coelurosaurs

Coelurosaurs were typically slender meat-eaters with small heads, long necks and long grasping arms.

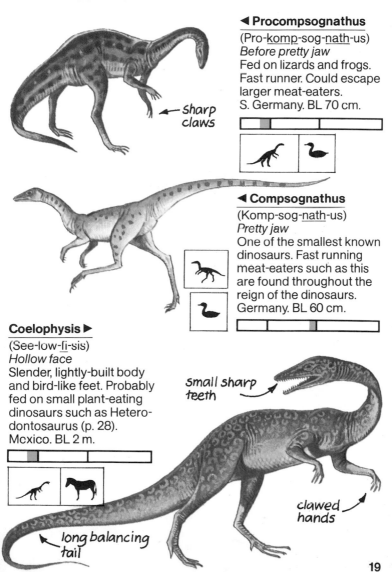

◄ Procompsognathus
(Pro-<u>komp</u>-sog-<u>nath</u>-us)
Before pretty jaw
Fed on lizards and frogs.
Fast runner. Could escape
larger meat-eaters.
S. Germany. BL 70 cm.

← *sharp claws*

◄ Compsognathus
(Komp-sog-<u>nath</u>-us)
Pretty jaw
One of the smallest known
dinosaurs. Fast running
meat-eaters such as this
are found throughout the
reign of the dinosaurs.
Germany. BL 60 cm.

Coelophysis ►
(See-low-<u>fi</u>-sis)
Hollow face
Slender, lightly-built body
and bird-like feet. Probably
fed on small plant-eating
dinosaurs such as Hetero-
dontosaurus (p. 28).
Mexico. BL 2 m.

small sharp teeth

clawed hands

long balancing tail

19

Coelurus ▶

(See-<u>lure</u>-us) *Hollow tail*
Agile flesh-eater. Had long
arms with sharp claws for
catching prey. May have
fed on Compsognathus
(p.19) and Archaeopteryx
(p.46). S. Germany. BL 2 m.

bird-like feet

◀ Velociraptor

(Vell-ossi-<u>rap</u>-tor)
Speedy predator
Fed on small reptiles or
mammals. One remark-
able fossil has been found
of Velociraptor and
Protoceratops in a
death struggle.
Mongolia. BL 1.5 m.

Saurornithoides ▶

(Sore-or-nith-<u>oy</u>-dees)
Bird-like reptile
Looks rather ostrich-like.
Its large eyes could have
given it good night vision.
May have fed on small
mammals.
Mongolia. BL 2-3 m.

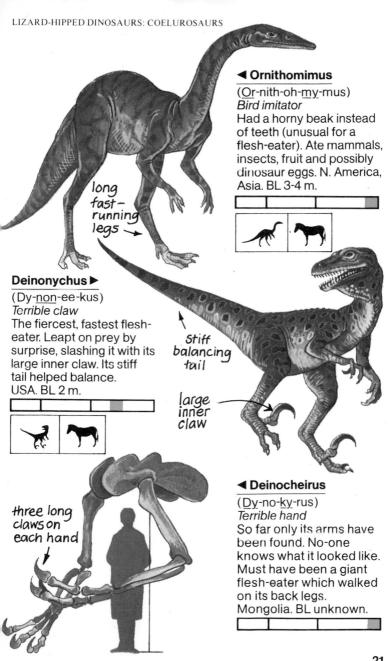

long
fast-
running
legs →

◀ Ornithomimus

(<u>Or</u>-nith-oh-<u>my</u>-mus)
Bird imitator
Had a horny beak instead
of teeth (unusual for a
flesh-eater). Ate mammals,
insects, fruit and possibly
dinosaur eggs. N. America,
Asia. BL 3-4 m.

Deinonychus ▶

(Dy-<u>non</u>-ee-kus)
Terrible claw
The fiercest, fastest flesh-
eater. Leapt on prey by
surprise, slashing it with its
large inner claw. Its stiff
tail helped balance.
USA. BL 2 m.

stiff
balancing
tail

large
inner
claw

three long
claws on
each hand

◀ Deinocheirus

(<u>Dy</u>-no-<u>ky</u>-rus)
Terrible hand
So far only its arms have
been found. No-one
knows what it looked like.
Must have been a giant
flesh-eater which walked
on its back legs.
Mongolia. BL unknown.

Carnosaurs

Carnosaurs were meat-eating dinosaurs and were large and bulky. They mainly had large heads, short necks and reduced arms. They killed their prey with their teeth or feet.

bony crests

◀ Dilophosaurus
(Dy-<u>loaf</u>-oh-<u>saw</u>-rus)
Two-crested reptile
One of the earliest carnosaurs. Had long, powerful legs and quite short arms. No-one knows why it had the two crests on its head. USA. BL 6 m.

Allosaurus ▶
(<u>Al</u>-oh-<u>saw</u>-rus)
Foreign reptile
This huge carnosaur hunted giant sauropods like the Apatosaurus and Diplodocus (p. 26). An Apatosaurus skeleton has been found with Allosaurus toothmarks on it.
N. America. BL 10 m.

sail →

◄ Spinosaurus
(<u>Spine</u>-oh-<u>saw</u>-rus)
Spiny reptile
Unusual carnosaur. Spines on its back (some up to 2 m long) formed a "sail". This helped to control its body temperature. Egypt. BL 8 m.

Megalosaurus ►
(<u>Mega</u>-low-<u>saw</u>-rus)
Giant reptile
Was the first dinosaur ever to be named and described (1824). It is a typical carnosaur. S. England. BL 6 m.

◄ Ceratosaurus
(Ser-<u>at</u>-oh-<u>saw</u>-rus)
Horned reptile
Had a small horn on top of its head and bony ridges over its eyes. N. America. BL 6 m.

23

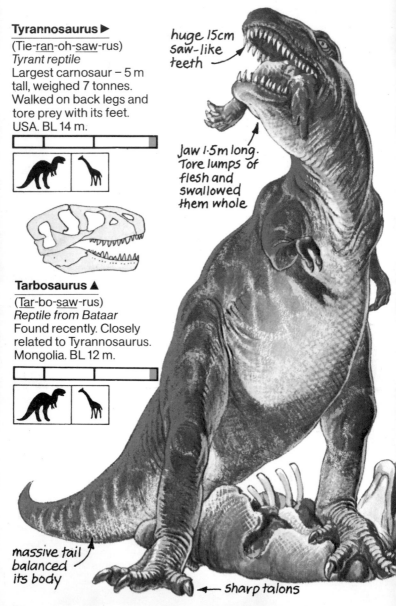

Tyrannosaurus ▶

(Tie-<u>ran</u>-oh-<u>saw</u>-rus)
Tyrant reptile
Largest carnosaur – 5 m
tall, weighed 7 tonnes.
Walked on back legs and
tore prey with its feet.
USA. BL 14 m.

Tarbosaurus ▲

(<u>Tar</u>-bo-<u>saw</u>-rus)
Reptile from Bataar
Found recently. Closely
related to Tyrannosaurus.
Mongolia. BL 12 m.

huge 15cm
saw-like
teeth

Jaw 1.5m long.
Tore lumps of
flesh and
swallowed
them whole

massive tail
balanced
its body

sharp talons

Prosauropods

Prosauropods were moderate to large plant-eating dinosaurs which lived in late Triassic times. They have the same ancestors as the huge plant-eating sauropods of the Jurassic Period (see overleaf).

Melanorosaurus ▶

(Mel-<u>an</u>-or-oh-<u>saw</u>-rus)
Black reptile
Bulky, heavy plant-eater. Walked on all fours, its great weight supported by massive pillar-like legs and powerful feet. S. Africa. BL 10 m or more.

long neck →

Plateosaurus ▼

(Plat-ee-oh-<u>saw</u>-rus)
Flat reptile
Lived in herds. Normally walked on all fours. Could stand on back legs with neck outstretched to reach leaves on trees. Its teeth were small and leaf-shaped. S. Germany. BL 6 m.

curved claws used for defence

Sauropods

Sauropods lived in Jurassic and Cretaceous times. They had huge bodies, long necks and even longer tails. They could feed only on soft plants as their teeth were weak and peg-like.

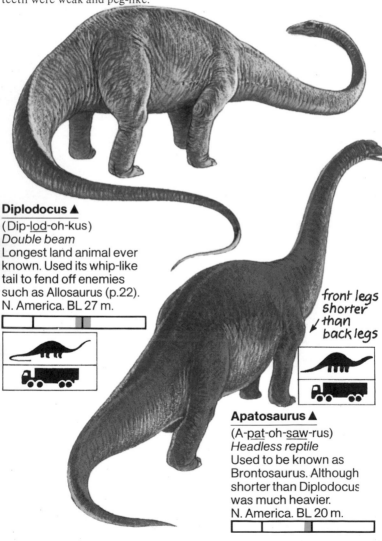

Diplodocus ▲

(Dip-<u>lod</u>-oh-kus)
Double beam
Longest land animal ever known. Used its whip-like tail to fend off enemies such as Allosaurus (p.22). N. America. BL 27 m.

front legs
shorter
than
back legs

Apatosaurus ▲

(A-<u>pat</u>-oh-<u>saw</u>-rus)
Headless reptile
Used to be known as Brontosaurus. Although shorter than Diplodocus was much heavier.
N. America. BL 20 m.

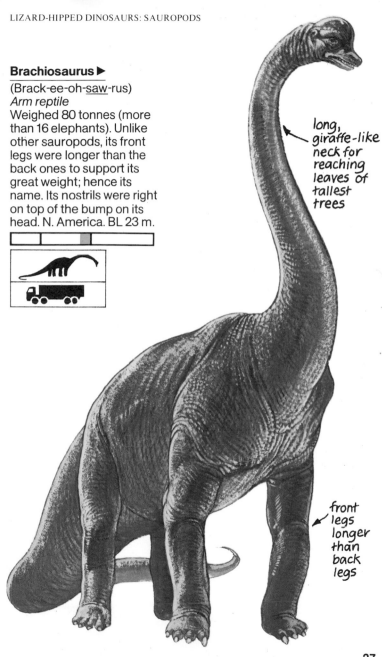

Brachiosaurus ▶

(Brack-ee-oh-<u>saw</u>-rus)
Arm reptile
Weighed 80 tonnes (more than 16 elephants). Unlike other sauropods, its front legs were longer than the back ones to support its great weight; hence its name. Its nostrils were right on top of the bump on its head. N. America. BL 23 m.

long, giraffe-like neck for reaching leaves of tallest trees

front legs longer than back legs

27

Ornithopods

Ornithopods had bird-like feet and walked mainly on their back legs. They were all plant-eaters and had a bird-like, horny beak for nipping off food.

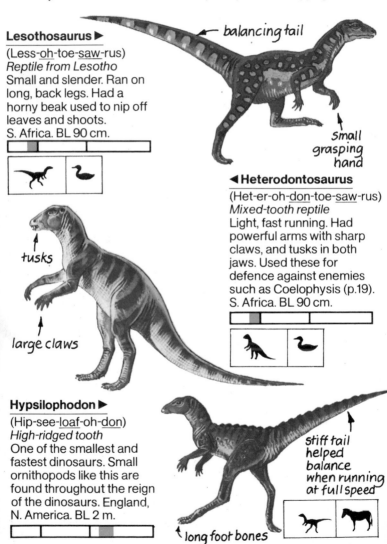

Lesothosaurus ▶
(Less-<u>oh</u>-toe-<u>saw</u>-rus)
Reptile from Lesotho
Small and slender. Ran on long, back legs. Had a horny beak used to nip off leaves and shoots.
S. Africa. BL 90 cm.

balancing tail

small grasping hand

◀ Heterodontosaurus
(Het-er-oh-<u>don</u>-toe-<u>saw</u>-rus)
Mixed-tooth reptile
Light, fast running. Had powerful arms with sharp claws, and tusks in both jaws. Used these for defence against enemies such as Coelophysis (p.19).
S. Africa. BL 90 cm.

tusks

large claws

Hypsilophodon ▶
(Hip-see-<u>loaf</u>-oh-<u>don</u>)
High-ridged tooth
One of the smallest and fastest dinosaurs. Small ornithopods like this are found throughout the reign of the dinosaurs. England, N. America. BL 2 m.

stiff tail helped balance when running at full speed

long foot bones

28

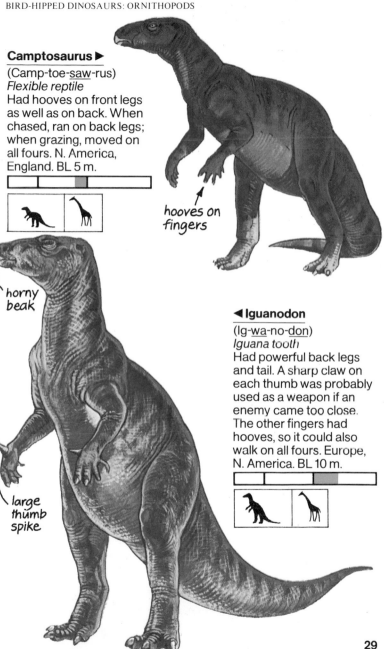

Camptosaurus ▶

(Camp-toe-<u>saw</u>-rus)
Flexible reptile
Had hooves on front legs
as well as on back. When
chased, ran on back legs;
when grazing, moved on
all fours. N. America,
England. BL 5 m.

hooves on
fingers

horny
beak

◀ Iguanodon

(Ig-<u>wa</u>-no-<u>don</u>)
Iguana tooth
Had powerful back legs
and tail. A sharp claw on
each thumb was probably
used as a weapon if an
enemy came too close.
The other fingers had
hooves, so it could also
walk on all fours. Europe,
N. America. BL 10 m.

large
thumb
spike

29

Duck-billed dinosaurs

Duck-billed dinosaurs were descended from animals like Iguanodon (see page 29). They lived in late Cretaceous times and are also known as hadrosaurs. Their top jaw was flattened at the tip and looked like a duck's bill – hence their popular name. Their teeth were small, ridged and closely packed, and could grind tough, woody plants.

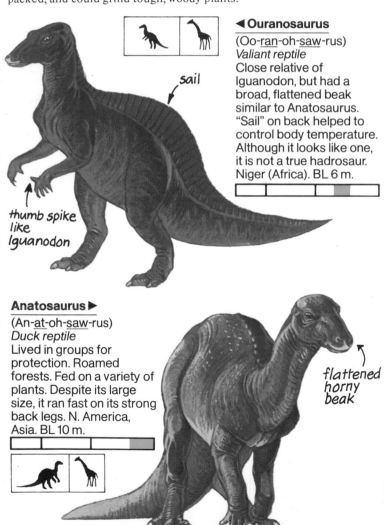

sail

thumb spike like Iguanodon

◀ Ouranosaurus

(Oo-<u>ran</u>-oh-<u>saw</u>-rus)
Valiant reptile
Close relative of Iguanodon, but had a broad, flattened beak similar to Anatosaurus. "Sail" on back helped to control body temperature. Although it looks like one, it is not a true hadrosaur. Niger (Africa). BL 6 m.

Anatosaurus ▶

(An-<u>at</u>-oh-<u>saw</u>-rus)
Duck reptile
Lived in groups for protection. Roamed forests. Fed on a variety of plants. Despite its large size, it ran fast on its strong back legs. N. America, Asia. BL 10 m.

flattened horny beak

Although the bodies of most hadrosaurs are practically identical in shape, the head of each species is very distinctive.

bump on nose ↙

◀ Kritosaurus

(Krit-oh-<u>saw</u>-rus)
Reptile from Kirtland
Had a flat head with a hump on its nose. This may have been used for butting rivals in the mating season. Kirtland, USA. BL 10 m.

Saurolophus ▶

(Saw-rol-<u>oh</u>-fuss)
Ridged reptile
Had a prong on the back of its head. One suggestion is that this supported inflatable nose pouches so that the animal could bellow at rivals. N. America, Mongolia. BL 10 m.

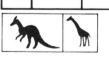

prong →

◀ Tsintaosaurus

(<u>Sin</u>-ta-oh-<u>saw</u>-rus)
Reptile from Tsintao
Had a long, solid, bony spike, turned forward, on the top of its head. This may have been used as a weapon as well as supporting its nose pouches. China. BL 10 m.

Edmontosaurus ▶

(Ed-mon-toe-saw-rus)
Reptile from Edmonton
Flat-headed. Had an
extremely broad spoon-
like beak. The pouches
round its nostrils may have
been inflatable. Canada.
BL 10 m.

◀ Corythosaurus

(Ko-rith-oh-saw-rus)
Helmeted reptile
There were complex
passages inside its deep
crest. It may be that these
allowed the dinosaur to
have a strong sense of
smell. N. America. BL 10 m.

helmet-
like
crest

2m

◀ Parasaurolophus

(Para-saw-ro-loh-fuss)
*Reptile with parallel-sided
crest*
Its hollow crest had
complex air passages. It
was once thought this was
used like a snorkel for
feeding underwater.
N. America. BL 10 m.

Dome-headed dinosaurs

These dome-headed dinosaurs were closely related to ornithopods (see page 28). They had similar bodies and were also bird-hipped plant-eaters. The dome of their skull was, however, extraordinarily thick. They lived in late Cretaceous times and are known as pachycephalosaurs.

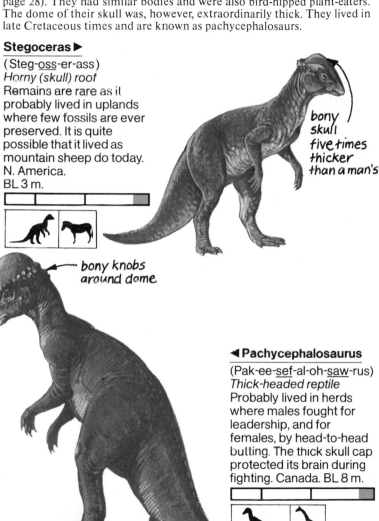

Stegoceras ▶

(Steg-<u>oss</u>-er-ass)
Horny (skull) roof
Remains are rare as it probably lived in uplands where few fossils are ever preserved. It is quite possible that it lived as mountain sheep do today. N. America.
BL 3 m.

bony skull five times thicker than a man's

bony knobs around dome

◀ Pachycephalosaurus

(Pak-ee-<u>sef</u>-al-oh-<u>saw</u>-rus)
Thick-headed reptile
Probably lived in herds where males fought for leadership, and for females, by head-to-head butting. The thick skull cap protected its brain during fighting. Canada. BL 8 m.

Horned dinosaurs

These generally large, heavy, horned dinosaurs with parrot-like beaks lived in late Cretaceous times. They are known as ceratopians and were particularly common in North America. Most of them can be distinguished by the size and shape of their horns and neck frill.

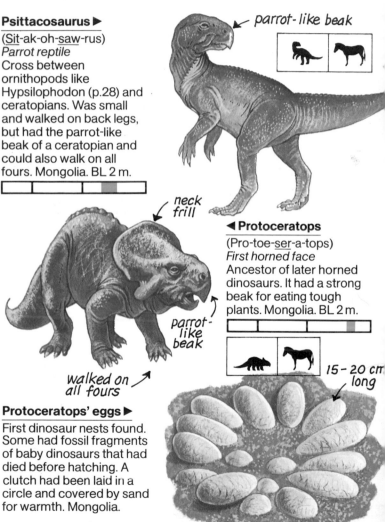

Psittacosaurus ▶

(<u>Sit</u>-ak-oh-<u>saw</u>-rus)
Parrot reptile
Cross between ornithopods like Hypsilophodon (p.28) and ceratopians. Was small and walked on back legs, but had the parrot-like beak of a ceratopian and could also walk on all fours. Mongolia. BL 2 m.

parrot-like beak

neck frill

◀ Protoceratops

(Pro-toe-<u>ser</u>-a-tops)
First horned face
Ancestor of later horned dinosaurs. It had a strong beak for eating tough plants. Mongolia. BL 2 m.

parrot-like beak

walked on all fours

15 – 20 cm long

Protoceratops' eggs ▶

First dinosaur nests found. Some had fossil fragments of baby dinosaurs that had died before hatching. A clutch had been laid in a circle and covered by sand for warmth. Mongolia.

Monoclonius ▶

(<u>Mon</u>-oh-<u>clo</u>-nee-us)
Single shoot
Looked similar to present-day rhinoceros. Had a single horn on nose and very small eyebrow ridges. Lived in herds.
N. America. BL 8 m.

◀ Pentaceratops

(<u>Pent</u>-ah-<u>ser</u>-a-tops)
Five-horned face
Its large frill extended half-way down its back. Apart from its nose and eyebrow horns it also had two pointed cheek bones, like horns, beneath its eyes. N. America. BL 7 m.

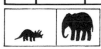

pointed
cheek
bones

35

Pachyrhinosaurus ▶

(Pack-ee-<u>rye</u>-no-<u>saw</u>-rus)
Thick-nosed reptile
A hornless ceratopian with a short frill. It had a thick pad of bone on top of its nose, between its eyes. Canada. BL 4 m.

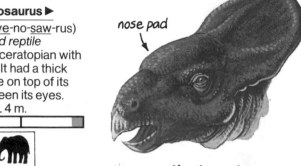
nose pad

◀ Leptoceratops

(<u>Lep</u>-toe-<u>ser</u>-a-tops)
Slender-horned face
Unusual ceratopian. Small and agile, it ran on its back legs. Its frill was small and it had no horns, as it could run to escape predators rather than using horns to defend itself.
N. America. BL 2 m.

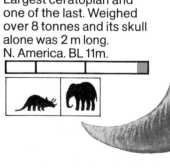

Triceratops ▶

(Try-<u>ser</u>-a-tops)
Three-horned face
Largest ceratopian and one of the last. Weighed over 8 tonnes and its skull alone was 2 m long.
N. America. BL 11m.

horns
1m long

Plated dinosaurs

Stegosaurs were large plant-eating dinosaurs that lived in late Jurassic times. They can be easily recognized because they had large, bony plates sticking out of the skin on their backs.

Kentrosaurus ▶

(<u>Ken</u>-tro-<u>saw</u>-rus)
Prickly reptile
In danger, it would probably have turned its back on a predator. The spiky tail would have made attack difficult.
Tanzania. BL 5 m.

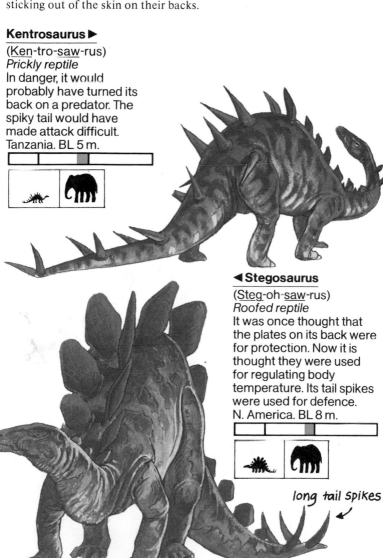

◀ Stegosaurus

(<u>Steg</u>-oh-<u>saw</u>-rus)
Roofed reptile
It was once thought that the plates on its back were for protection. Now it is thought they were used for regulating body temperature. Its tail spikes were used for defence.
N. America. BL 8 m.

long tail spikes

37

Armoured dinosaurs

Armoured dinosaurs were quite large, slow-moving, plant-eaters. They lived in late Jurassic and Cretaceous times and are known as ankylosaurs.

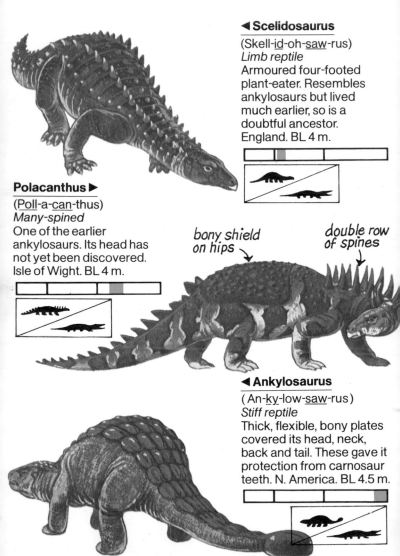

◄ Scelidosaurus
(Skell-<u>id</u>-oh-<u>saw</u>-rus)
Limb reptile
Armoured four-footed plant-eater. Resembles ankylosaurs but lived much earlier, so is a doubtful ancestor. England. BL 4 m.

Polacanthus ▶
(<u>Poll</u>-a-<u>can</u>-thus)
Many-spined
One of the earlier ankylosaurs. Its head has not yet been discovered. Isle of Wight. BL 4 m.

bony shield on hips ↘

double row of spines ↘

◄ Ankylosaurus
(An-<u>ky</u>-low-<u>saw</u>-rus)
Stiff reptile
Thick, flexible, bony plates covered its head, neck, back and tail. These gave it protection from carnosaur teeth. N. America. BL 4.5 m.

bony armour with spikes cover body from nose to tail

walked with sprawling gait to support its weight

◄ Euoplocephalus

(Yew-oh-plo-<u>sef</u>-al-us)
True-plated head
Weighed up to 5 tonnes.
In danger, it squatted to
protect its soft belly and
drew its head close to its
body. N. America. BL 7 m.

Nodosaurus ►

(<u>Noh</u>-doh-<u>saw</u>-rus)
Lumpy lizard
Flexible armour plating
covered its back and sides.
It does not seem to have
a tail club like other
ankylosaurs. N. America.
BL 6 m.

possibly swung tail at attackers ➔

◄ Paleoscincus

(Pay-lee-oh-<u>skink</u>-us)
Ancient lizard
Low-slung body and short
legs. Sharp spikes stuck
out at edges of armour.
This prevented predators
attacking its legs or belly.
N. America. BL 6 m.

39

Flying reptiles

Pterosaurs were light, fragile reptiles that took to the air. Their wings were leathery membranes stretched out along enormously elongated arms and fingers (or, as in one case below, along the legs). They may have evolved from small distant relatives of Euparkeria (see page 18).

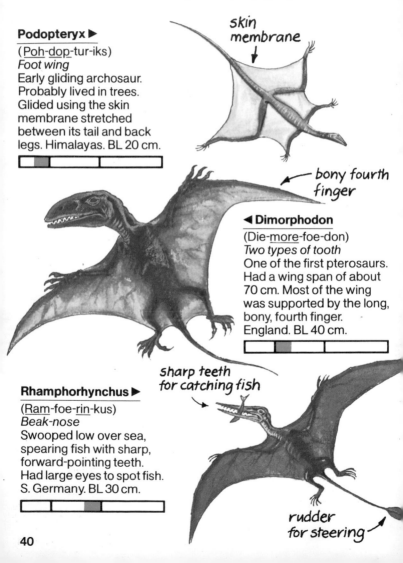

Podopteryx ▶

(Poh-dop-tur-iks)
Foot wing
Early gliding archosaur. Probably lived in trees. Glided using the skin membrane stretched between its tail and back legs. Himalayas. BL 20 cm.

skin membrane

bony fourth finger

◀ Dimorphodon

(Die-more-foe-don)
Two types of tooth
One of the first pterosaurs. Had a wing span of about 70 cm. Most of the wing was supported by the long, bony, fourth finger. England. BL 40 cm.

Rhamphorhynchus ▶

(Ram-foe-rin-kus)
Beak-nose
Swooped low over sea, spearing fish with sharp, forward-pointing teeth. Had large eyes to spot fish. S. Germany. BL 30 cm.

sharp teeth for catching fish

rudder for steering

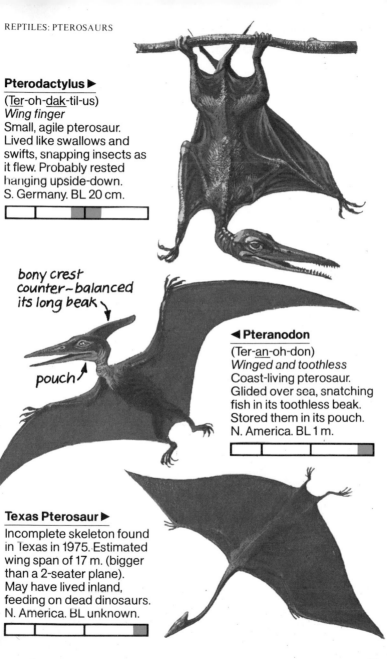

Pterodactylus ▶
(<u>Ter</u>-oh-<u>dak</u>-til-us)
Wing finger
Small, agile pterosaur.
Lived like swallows and
swifts, snapping insects as
it flew. Probably rested
hanging upside-down.
S. Germany. BL 20 cm.

*bony crest
counter-balanced
its long beak* ↘

pouch ↗

◀ Pteranodon
(Ter-<u>an</u>-oh-don)
Winged and toothless
Coast-living pterosaur.
Glided over sea, snatching
fish in its toothless beak.
Stored them in its pouch.
N. America. BL 1 m.

Texas Pterosaur ▶
Incomplete skeleton found
in Texas in 1975. Estimated
wing span of 17 m. (bigger
than a 2-seater plane).
May have lived inland,
feeding on dead dinosaurs.
N. America. BL unknown.

Phytosaurs and crocodiles

Phytosaurs (such as Rutiodon below) were primitive, crocodile-like archosaurs which lived at the end of the Triassic Period. Crocodiles and alligators, as we know them today, are an ancient group dating back to relatives like Protosuchus, an early true crocodile.

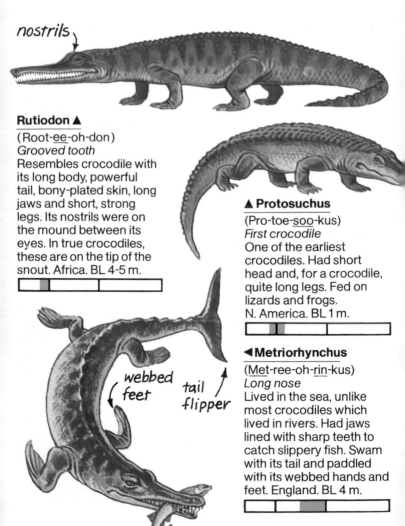

nostrils

Rutiodon ▲

(Root-<u>ee</u>-oh-don)
Grooved tooth
Resembles crocodile with its long body, powerful tail, bony-plated skin, long jaws and short, strong legs. Its nostrils were on the mound between its eyes. In true crocodiles, these are on the tip of the snout. Africa. BL 4-5 m.

▲ Protosuchus

(Pro-toe-<u>soo</u>-kus)
First crocodile
One of the earliest crocodiles. Had short head and, for a crocodile, quite long legs. Fed on lizards and frogs.
N. America. BL 1 m.

◄ Metriorhynchus

(<u>Met</u>-ree-oh-<u>rin</u>-kus)
Long nose
Lived in the sea, unlike most crocodiles which lived in rivers. Had jaws lined with sharp teeth to catch slippery fish. Swam with its tail and paddled with its webbed hands and feet. England. BL 4 m.

webbed feet

tail flipper

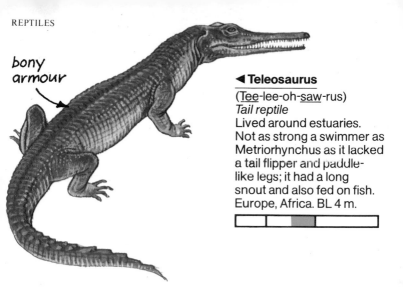

bony armour

◄ Teleosaurus

(<u>Tee</u>-lee-oh-<u>saw</u>-rus)
Tail reptile
Lived around estuaries.
Not as strong a swimmer as
Metriorhynchus as it lacked
a tail flipper and paddle-
like legs; it had a long
snout and also fed on fish.
Europe, Africa. BL 4 m.

Bernissartia ►

(<u>Bur</u>-nee-<u>sar</u>-tee-ah)
*Dwarf crocodile from
Bernissart*
Its remains were found
among Iguanodon
skeletons. Its blunt teeth
show it may have fed on
shellfish or perhaps on
dead animals. Belgium,
England. BL 60 cm.

blunt teeth

only a skull has been found

◄ Deinosuchus

(<u>Dy</u>-no-<u>soo</u>-kus)
Terrible crocodile
Lived in the age of
dinosaurs. Giant estuarine
crocodile. Its head was
over 2 m long. It may have
fed on dinosaurs.
N. America. BL 15 m.

Swimming reptiles

Several kinds of sea-going reptiles lived in the same Era, the Mesozoic, as the dinosaurs. Ichthyosaurs (fish-reptiles) resembled mammalian dolphins of today. Plesiosaurs, pliosaurs and nothosaurs were less fish-like.

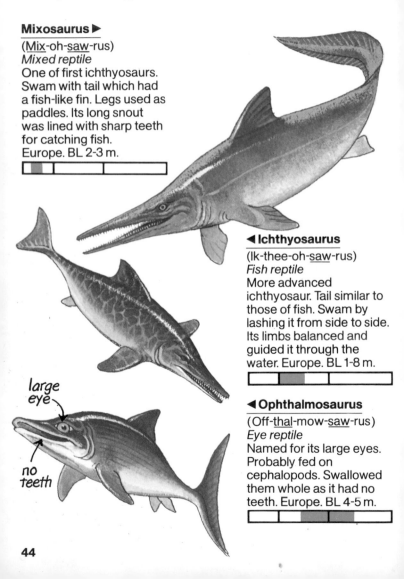

Mixosaurus ▶

(<u>Mix</u>-oh-<u>saw</u>-rus)
Mixed reptile
One of first ichthyosaurs.
Swam with tail which had
a fish-like fin. Legs used as
paddles. Its long snout
was lined with sharp teeth
for catching fish.
Europe. BL 2-3 m.

◀ Ichthyosaurus

(Ik-thee-oh-<u>saw</u>-rus)
Fish reptile
More advanced
ichthyosaur. Tail similar to
those of fish. Swam by
lashing it from side to side.
Its limbs balanced and
guided it through the
water. Europe. BL 1-8 m.

◀ Ophthalmosaurus

(Off-<u>thal</u>-mow-<u>saw</u>-rus)
Eye reptile
Named for its large eyes.
Probably fed on
cephalopods. Swallowed
them whole as it had no
teeth. Europe. BL 4-5 m.

large
eye

no
teeth

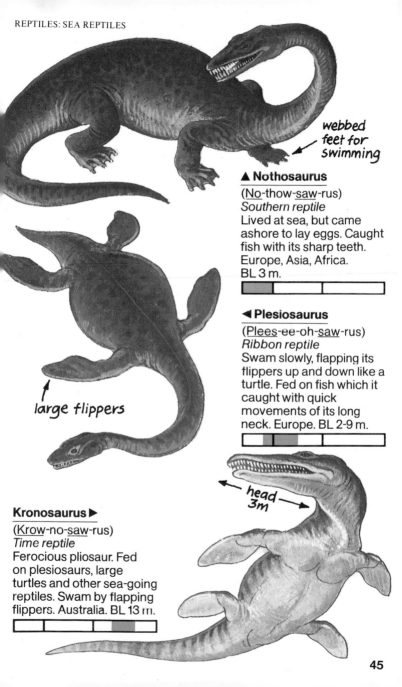

webbed feet for swimming

▲ Nothosaurus

(<u>No</u>-thow-<u>saw</u>-rus)
Southern reptile
Lived at sea, but came ashore to lay eggs. Caught fish with its sharp teeth. Europe, Asia, Africa. BL 3 m.

◄ Plesiosaurus

(<u>Plees</u>-ee-oh-<u>saw</u>-rus)
Ribbon reptile
Swam slowly, flapping its flippers up and down like a turtle. Fed on fish which it caught with quick movements of its long neck. Europe. BL 2-9 m.

large flippers

head 3m

Kronosaurus ►

(<u>Krow</u>-no-<u>saw</u>-rus)
Time reptile
Ferocious pliosaur. Fed on plesiosaurs, large turtles and other sea-going reptiles. Swam by flapping flippers. Australia. BL 13 m.

The earliest bird

Archaeopteryx ▶

(Are-kee-op-tur-iks)
Ancient wing
First skeleton found in
Germany in 1861. Even the
feathers on wings and
body were preserved. Had
teeth, long, bony tail and
wing claws. Probably could
not fly strongly as had no
large breast bone to which
flight muscles could attach.
Modern birds evolved from
it. Europe. BL 20 cm.

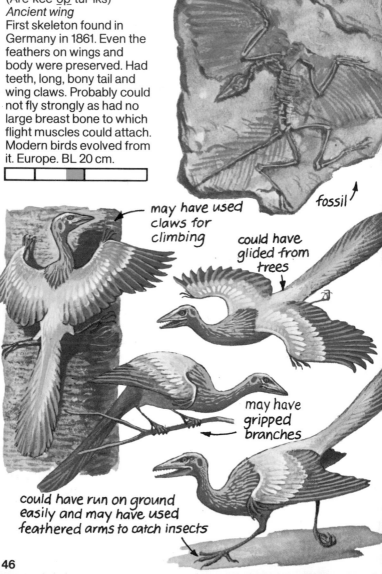

fossil

may have used
claws for
climbing

could have
glided from
trees

may have
gripped
branches

could have run on ground
easily and may have used
feathered arms to catch insects

Mammal origins

During the Triassic Period, another great group of animals, the mammals (our ancestors), first started to make their appearance. They evolved from some mammal-like reptiles.

Cynognathus ▶

(<u>Sine</u>-og-<u>nath</u>-us)
Dog jaw
As its name suggests, it had a dog-like look. Like mammals, it had several different types of teeth (a reptile's teeth are usually all of the same type). Africa. BL 2 m.

scaly skin

hairy skin

◀ Thrinaxodon

(Thrin-<u>axe</u>-oh-don)
Trident tooth
Even more mammal-like than Cynognathus. Had teeth of different kinds. Had whiskers on its nose, and was probably hairy like a mammal. S. Africa.
BL 40 cm.

Megazostrodon ▶

(<u>Meg</u>-ah-<u>zost</u>-ro-don)
Big girdle tooth
Earliest true mammal. Was hairy, warm-blooded and gave birth to live young. Was tiny and shrew-like. It fed on insects and grubs. S. Africa.
BL 6-8 cm.

large mobile ears

thick fur

Fossils

Fossil fern ▶

Fern fronds are often found in coal measures of Carboniferous times. They are common plants of this Period, often found alongside early amphibians. Can be identified only if the seed-bearing structure is present.

tentacles

limestone cup

◀ Cup coral

These early corals lived in individual, cup-shaped limestone structures which rested on the sea floor. They were the oldest coral animals, surviving from ancient times right through the age of dinosaurs. Now replaced by reef corals.

hole for stalk

Brachiopods ▶

(<u>Brack</u>-ee-oh-pods)
Lamp shells
Commonest fossil, found in all rocks from early Cambrian to recent times. Attached by a stalk to the sea bed, they lived inside a hinged shell and filtered food particles from the water.

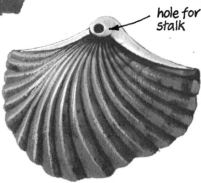

Gastropods ▶

Molluscs, such as snails, have been common for millions of years since Cambrian times. The shells in which they lived vary in shape – they may be coiled like a catherine wheel or in a spiral, or be cone-shaped like a limpet.

limpet

whelk →

◀ Bivalves

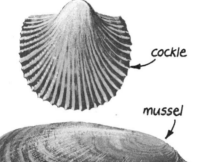

cockle

mussel

These molluscs are so-called because they live inside two shells (called valves) which are hinged together. This group includes cockles, mussels and razor shells. They are common fossils. In some cases great thicknesses of rock are made entirely of bivalve shells.

Ammonite ▶

Belonged to the cephalopod group of molluscs, which also includes octopuses and squids. Were common in seas until the late Cretaceous Period, then became extinct. The coiled shell contained chambers filled with air, which helped the animal float.

Trilobite ▶
(<u>Try</u>-low-<u>bite</u>)
Three-lobed
Had a hard outer shell and many jointed legs. Most scavenged for food on the sea floor. Some could swim and burrow.

◀ Crinoid
(Crin-oyd)
Sea lily
Related to starfish and sea urchins. Lived attached to sea floor by a long stalk. Had a squat body and long tentacles for catching plankton.

Vertebrate fossils ▶
Fossils of back-boned animals that lived on land or in the air are rarer than those of sea animals. Sometimes a complete skeleton is discovered, but mainly just an odd tooth or bone is found. These may be difficult to identify.

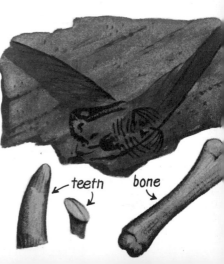

teeth *bone*

Living fossils

◀ Tuatara

Living relative of lizard-like animals numerous in Triassic times. Very rare. Found in sparsely inhabited islands near New Zealand. Appearance has hardly changed in 200 million years.

◀ Pearly Nautilus

Rare. Distant living relative of squids, octopuses and extinct ammonites. Lives in a coiled shell which acts as a buoyancy tank, so it can float at any level. Found in the Indian Ocean.

Coelacanth ▶

(See-la-canth)
Hollow spine
Large, predatory fish. Lives in deep waters off the Comoro Islands in the Indian Ocean. Can be traced back to Devonian Period. Relatives of ancient coelacanths include Eusthenopteron (p.15).

Brachiopods ▶

Found in coastal areas. Live inside two hinged shells. Have a long stalk attached to the sea floor Can be traced back to Cambrian Period.

Fossil collecting

Fossils are found in sedimentary rocks, such as clays, sandstone, mudstones, shales and limestones. To find rocks of this type in your area go to your nearest library or museum and ask to see the local geological guides. These often show exactly where various types of rock are found and what sorts of fossils are usually found in them.

The best places to look are those where the rock is clean and exposed and not covered by plants – such as cliffs by the sea, quarries, or where road workers have dug into hillsides. However, all these places can be dangerous. Without any covering of plants, rock tends to weather quickly and become unsafe, causing rockfalls or landslides. NEVER explore in these places alone and NEVER explore if you see a notice saying that an area is unsafe.

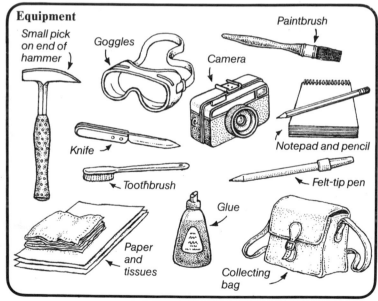

Equipment

Small pick on end of hammer

Goggles

Paintbrush

Camera

Knife

Notepad and pencil

Toothbrush

Felt-tip pen

Glue

Paper and tissues

Collecting bag

Recording your finds
Ideally, when you find a fossil, you should photograph it in position. Write in your notebook exactly where and when you found it. Your notes should make it possible for not only you, but anyone else, to find the exact spot.

JULY 15th.
Fossil tooth.
Cliffs near
Dover.
Position:
1m above
foot of cliff –
150m west
of steps.

Handling fossils

Clean the surface of the fossil with a brush. If it is small and can be moved easily, lift it along with the rock that surrounds it. In some cases you may need to free a fossil from a larger piece of rock. If the rock is soft (as are some clays and limestones) cut away the rock from beneath the fossil with a knife. If the rock is hard, you may need to use the hammer and chisel to free the fossil.

Wrap fossils carefully in tissues and paper and label each one before you put it in your collecting bag.

Both your field notes and the rock sample may be almost as important as the fossil. They can help a scientist to give a precise age to the fossil.

If you should find a very large fossil, it is best not to try to remove it yourself for fear of damaging it. Removing large fossils is a skilled job best left to experts from museums.

If you are unable to identify a fossil by yourself or from books, take or send it with your field notes to a museum, where someone should be able to identify it for you.

Keeping your collection

Each fossil that you collect should be stored separately with its own label and field notes. Any container – from a shoe box to a glass cabinet – will do, provided that it has a lid to keep out the dust.

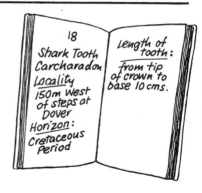

18
Shark Tooth
Carcharadon
Locality
150m West
of steps at
Dover
Horizon:
Cretaceous
Period

Length of
tooth:
from tip
of crown to
base 10 cms.

Ideally, you should also keep a catalogue of your collection. Give each fossil a collection number which you paint on its under surface. Enter the number in your catalogue, together with all the details about the fossil. Write down its name and where you found it. If you use a page for each fossil, there will be space left for you to describe other details as you find out more about them.

If your collection is large enough, you may find it best to divide your fossils into groups, depending on the kind of fossils they are – such as plant fossils, fish, shellfish, reptiles, mammals and others.

You may be interested to know that fossil collections of large museums in most countries have largely been founded by collections given to them by interested fossil collectors like you.

Fossil expeditions

1. Expeditions often go to quite remote parts of the world in search of fossils. A trained eye is needed to spot them. In the photograph, a large skeleton is buried in the rock face just below the matchbox. The clue was the end of the ribs seen poking out of the rock.

2. The first task of the palaeontologists (people who study fossils) is to remove most of the over-burden – this is the rock that lies above the skel-eton. The work is done with picks and shovels.

3. Then the delicate excavation can start. The last few centimetres of rock are carefully brushed and scraped away until the entire skeleton is exposed.

4. In preparation for its removal, the fossil is then excavated from beneath. It is left supported on narrow pillars of rock.

5. Finally, the fossil has to be divided into blocks so that it can be lifted. Each block is encased with layers of tissues and plaster-of-Paris bandages to prevent it from being damaged.

6. When the plaster has set, the blocks are labelled and lifted away. The entire plastered skeleton is transported back to a museum. There the bandages are removed. The fossil is cleaned carefully and prepared for study.

Two evolutionary problems

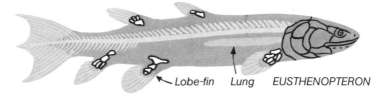

Lobe-fin   Lung   EUSTHENOPTERON

1. Out of the water and on to the land

Looking at a goldfish swimming in a pond, it is hard to imagine that a bony fish should ever try to crawl out of the water to seek another way of life on land. After all, a fish has no lungs to breathe air with and its frail fins could never support its body.

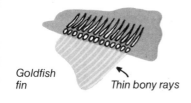

Goldfish fin

Thin bony rays

In the Devonian Period, however, there were fishes which were surprisingly well adapted to living on land. These fish (such as Eusthenopteron above) are often called lobe-finned fish, because their fins have thick muscular bases and a bony skeleton inside, so that they are rather like simple legs. These fish also had lungs for breathing air.

With simple, leg-like fins and lungs, these fish were able to leave the water and crawl on to the river banks. No-one really knows why a fish otherwise so well suited to living in water should try to live on land. There are many theories, however.

One possible answer is that the lobe-fins were forced to try and live on land. They lived in rivers and streams which had many large and ferocious fish. The small, young Eusthenopteron probably spent most of their early life in the shallow stream edges where larger fish could not reach them. If they did crowd into the shallows, it is not difficult to imagine them using their strong, lobed fins to haul themselves on to the river bank. There they could feed on the many insects and grubs which lived around the water's edge.

From these small beginnings the move to land was begun. Some lobe-fins became better adapted to life on land. Eventually, the early true land vertebrates, the amphibians such as Ichthyostega (below), appeared.

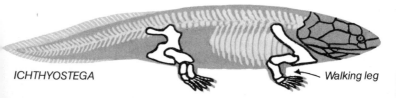

ICHTHYOSTEGA

Walking leg

2. Dinosaurs and birds

Another problem that has puzzled scientists for over a century is the origin of birds. They all agree that birds have evolved from reptiles, but the problem is to decide from which particular group of reptiles.

Archaeopteryx (see page 46) is the oldest bird fossil known. It has been studied by many different scientists, who each tried to decide which group of reptiles might be its closest relatives. Many people believe that Archaeopteryx is related to the ancestors of the dinosaurs, crocodiles and pterosaurs (animals such as Euparkeria).

Quite recently, however, it has been suggested that Archaeopteryx was a close relative of the coelurosaurian type of dinosaurs (see pages 19-21). In fact, one fossil skeleton of Archaeopteryx was mistaken for a coelurosaur for many years, because no feathers had been noticed – which goes to show how alike Archaeopteryx and the coelurosaurs are!

If Archaeopteryx does eventually prove to be a close relative of coelurosaurs, then it is amazing to think that the birds we see today are the closest living relatives of dinosaurs.

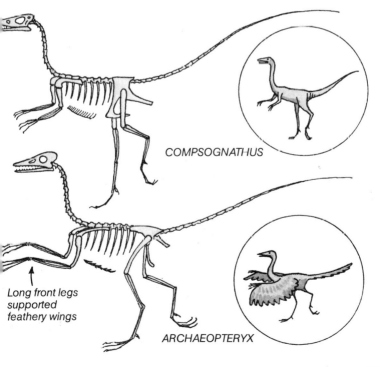

COMPSOGNATHUS

Long front legs supported feathery wings

ARCHAEOPTERYX

57

Why did dinosaurs disappear?

Sixty-four millon years ago, at the end of the Cretaceous Period, a puzzling thing happened. Up until this date, fossil remains of dinosaurs, giant sea reptiles (such as ichthyosaurs and plesiosaurs), flying reptiles (pterosaurs) and coiled shells of ammonites are found in rocks all over the world. After then, however, the rocks no longer contain any of these groups of animals. In their place are the fossilized remains of mammals, birds and a few surviving reptile groups such as lizards and snakes, crocodiles and turtles.

No-one really knows why certain groups of animals became extinct. There are, however, many theories about why dinosaurs died out. One suggestion is that small mammals which lived alongside the dinosaurs took to eating dinosaur eggs.

At first, mammals were not very numerous and ate relatively few eggs. Towards the end of the Cretaceous Period they became much more abundant and may have eaten so many eggs that dinosaurs died out.

Other theories consider the types of plants that existed at about the time that dinosaurs disappeared. In the early part of the Cretaceous Period, the most common types of plants were conifers, cycads and horsetails. These were probably the staple diet of plant-eating dinosaurs.

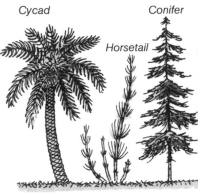

Cycad   Horsetail   Conifer

Towards the end of the Cretaceous Period, these plants were largely replaced by flowering plants. It has been suggested that either dinosaurs were unable to eat the tough, woody stems of these plants, or that they were poisoned by chemicals these plants produced, which dinosaurs could not taste.

Another suggestion is that the appearance of flowering plants, which often need insects to pollinate the flowers, encouraged a population explosion of butterflies and their larvae, caterpillars. The hungry caterpillars stripped all the plants bare, leaving nothing for the dinosaurs to eat. Without food, the dinosaurs thus died out.

◀ *Megazostrodon eating a dinosaur egg*

There is little evidence for any of these theories. Besides, none of them explains the disappearance of all the other animal groups.

There are two main theories which may be more likely. The first is that there was some sort of cosmic event – for example, the explosion of a star close to our solar system. This would have bathed the earth in deadly radiation. Animals on land would either have been killed by it or been so badly damaged that they could not give birth to live young afterwards.

Although the water would have shielded sea animals from much of the radiation, the surface layers containing plankton would have been badly affected. Life in the sea is very dependent on the plankton layers. If the plankton is killed, the chain of life in the sea is disrupted. Prehistoric fish fed on plankton and most of the large sea reptiles fed on fish. If the plankton had died, so would the fish and so, perhaps, would all the fish-eating reptiles.

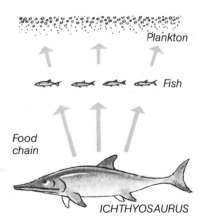

Plankton

Fish

Food chain

ICHTHYOSAURUS

The second theory is based on the movements of continents (see pages 5-7) and their effects on the climate. During the first half of the reign of dinosaurs, the continents were quite close together and the climate appears to have been warm.

During the Jurassic and the Cretaceous Periods, the continents started to separate. As they did so, the oceans opened up between them (as shown in the picture below). These large seaways produced much more changeable, colder conditions. At the end of the Cretaceous Period, the weather seems to have been rather cold.

In these new colder times, the dinosaurs would have been unable to keep their bodies warm, even if they were warm-blooded, because they had no fur or feathers to keep the heat in. Similarly, plankton in the sea would have been affected by these changing conditions. Many types of plankton are certainly known to have become extinct at this time. The pterosaurs may also have been affected by colder weather. They may have been close to extinction anyway. Birds were gradually replacing them throughout the Cretaceous Period.

Neither of these theories gives a whole answer. It may be that they are both quite wrong, but there is as yet no way to prove any of the answers!

Museum guide

Britain

The best exhibits of skeletons and reconstructed models of dinosaurs are at (1) the British Museum (Natural History) in London.

There are also examples of dinosaurs at:

2 Hancock Museum, Newcastle-upon-Tyne.
3 University Museum, Oxford.
4 University Museum of Zoology, Cambridge.

Many local museums have a collection of fossils and other prehistoric exhibits. Museums in the following towns and cities have good exhibits:

5 Belfast
6 Birmingham
7 Bristol
8 Cardiff
9 Edinburgh
10 Liverpool
11 Lyme Regis
12 Manchester
13 Sandown (Isle of Wight)
14 Sheffield

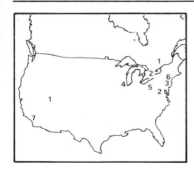

USA

1 Dinosaur National Monument, Utah.
  Dinosaur bones in the cliff face.
2 National Museum of Natural History, (Smithsonian Institute), Washington D.C.
3 American Museum of Natural History, New York.
4 Field Museum of Natural History, Chicago.
5 Carnegie Museum of Natural History, Pittsburgh.
6 Peabody Museum of Natural History, Yale University, New Haven.
7 Natural History Museum of Los Angeles County.

Canada

1 Canadian National Museum of Natural Sciences, Ottawa.
2 Royal Ontario Museum, Toronto.

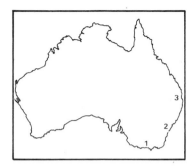

Australia

1 National Museum of Victoria, Melbourne.
2 Sydney Natural History Museum, Sydney.
3 Queensland Museum, Brisbane.

Europe

Belgium
1 Institut Royal des Sciences Naturelles de Belgique, Brussels.
France
2 Musée National d'Histoire Naturelle, Paris.
East Germany
3 Museum für Naturkunde, East Berlin.
West Germany
4 Senckenburg Museum, Frankfurt-am-Main.

Books to read

A New Look at the Dinosaurs. Alan Charig (Heinemann)
Prehistoric Animals. C. B. Cox (Hamlyn)
The Evolution and Ecology of Dinosaurs. L. B. Halstead (Peter Lowe)
The Age of Dinosaurs. B. Kurten (Weidenfeld and Nicholson)
All New Dinosaurs (and their friends). R. A. Long and S. P. Welles (Bellerophon Books)
A Natural History of Dinosaurs. R. T. J. Moody (Hamlyn)
Dinosaurs (in the Children's Picture Prehistory series). Anne McCord (Usborne)
Life Before Man. Z. V. Spinar and Z. Burian (Thames and Hudson)
The World of Dinosaurs. M. Tweedie (Weidenfeld and Nicholson)

Glossary

Adapt – to alter the structure of an organ so that it is better suited to the function that it has to perform.

Amphibian – a back-boned animal which lays soft, jelly-covered eggs (usually in water). Usually, tadpoles emerge from these eggs. Today's amphibians have soft, moist skin. Examples include frogs, toads, salamanders and newts.

Archosaur – group of reptiles which have a particular arrangement of holes in their skulls, and tend to draw their legs under their bodies. Archosaur means "ruling reptile". Examples include crocodiles, dinosaurs and pterosaurs.

Cephalopod – see Mollusc.

Coal measure – the layers of coal-bearing rocks laid down in the Carboniferous and Permian Periods. These rocks contain, among other things, remains of some of the earliest amphibians and reptiles.

"Cold-blooded" – generally refers to an animal which is unable to regulate its own body temperature. Thus, on a cold day the animal is cold, and on a warm day it is correspondingly warm. Living amphibians and reptiles are both cold-blooded.

Evolution – the process by which plants and animals can gradually, over many generations, alter their appearance and structure so that they are better suited to the conditions of their environment.

"Lobe-fin" – name given to the members of a group of ancient fish which had a muscular and bony base to their fins. Legs evolved from structures like these. Eusthenopteron, coelacanths and lung fish are all lobe-finned.

Mammal – a back-boned animal which gives birth to live young, suckles on its mother's milk, is warm-blooded, has hairy skin and grows only two sets of teeth (a milk and a permanent set).

Mollusc – a soft-bodied, hard-shelled animal. Examples include limpets, snails, cephalopods (nautiloids, octopuses, ammonites), and bivalves.

Palaeontologist – someone who studies fossils.

Palaeontology – the science of the study of fossils.

Predator – an animal which lives by killing and feeding (preying) on other animals.

Reptile – a back-boned animal which has a scaly skin, lays shelled eggs on land and is usually cold-blooded. Examples include lizards, snakes, crocodiles, turtles, tortoises and dinosaurs.

Scavenger – generally an animal which feeds on any food it happens to find. Often this term applies to animals which feed on the remains of a carcass that another animal has killed or partly eaten.

Sediment – fine particles of sand or clay that settle at the bottom of a lake or ocean.

Sedimentary rock – rock formed from compressed layers of sediment.

Vertebrate – an animal with a backbone. Examples include amphibians, fish, reptiles, birds and mammals.

"Warm-blooded" – generally refers to animals which can maintain a constant high body temperature and are therefore unaffected by outside conditions. Birds and mammals are both warm-blooded.

Index